You're It!

Tag, Red Rover, and Other Folk Games

North American Folklore for Youth

You're It!

Tag, Red Rover, and Other Folk Games

Thomas Arkham

Mason Crest

Mason Crest
370 Reed Road
Broomall, Pennsylvania 19008
www.masoncrest.com

Printed and bound in the United States of America.

First printing
9 8 7 6 5 4 3 2 1

Library of Congress Cataloging-in-Publication Data

Arkham, Thomas.
 You're it! tag, red rover, and other folk games / Thomas Arkham.
     p. cm.
 Includes index.
 ISBN 978-1-4222-2496-0 (hardcover) — ISBN 978-1-4222-2486-1
(hardcover series) — ISBN 978-1-4222-9261-7 (ebook)
 1. Games—Juvenile literature. 2. Folklore and children I. Title.
 GV1201.A78 2013
 790.1—dc23
                              2012013556

Produced by Harding House Publishing Services, Inc.
www.hardinghousepages.com
Cover design by Torque Advertising + Design.

Contents

# Introduction

by Dr. Alan Jabbour

What do a story, a joke, a fiddle tune, a quilt, a dance, a game of jacks, a holiday celebration, and a Halloween costume have in common? Not much, at first glance. But they're all part of the stuff we call "folklore."

The word "folklore" means the ways of thinking and acting that are learned and passed along by ordinary people. Folklore goes from grandparents to parents to children—and on to *their* children. It may be passed along in words, like the urban legend we hear from friends who promise us that it *really* happened to someone they know. Or it may be tunes or dance steps we pick up on the block where we live. It could be the quilt our aunt made. Much of the time we learn folklore without even knowing where or how we learned it.

Folklore is not something that's far away or long ago. It's something we use and enjoy every day! It is often ordinary—

and yet at the same time, it makes life seem very special. Folklore is the culture we share with others in our homes, our neighborhoods, and our places of worship. It helps tell us who we are.

Our first sense of who we are comes from our families. Family folklore—like eating certain meals together or prayers or songs—gives us a sense of belonging. But as we grow older we learn to belong to other groups as well. Maybe your family is Irish. Or maybe you live in a Hispanic neighborhood in New York City. Or you might live in the country in the middle of Iowa. Maybe you're a Catholic—or a Muslim—or you're Jewish. Each one of these groups to which you belong will have it's own folklore. A certain dance step may be African American. A story may have come from Germany. A hymn may be Protestant. A recipe may have been handed down by your Italian grandmother. All this folklore helps the people who belong to a certain group feel connected to each other.

Folklore can make each group special, different from all the others. But at the same time folklore is one of the best ways we can get to know to each other. We can learn about Vietnamese immigrants by eating Vietnamese foods. We can understand newcomers from Somalia by enjoying their music and dance. Stories, songs, and artwork move from group to group. And everyone is the richer!

Folklore isn't something you usually learn in school. Somebody, somewhere, taught you that jump-rope rhyme you know—but you probably can't remember *who* taught you. You definitely didn't learn it in a schoolbook, though! You can study folklore and learn about it—that's what you are doing now in this book!—but folklore normally is something that just gets passed along from person to person.

This series of books explores the many kinds folklore you can find across the North American continent. As you read, you'll learn something about yourself—and you'll learn about your neighbors as well!

ONE
Time for Fun

Do you remember playing Itsy-Bitsy Spider and Ring-Around-the-Rosie when you were very young? When you were a little bit older, you probably played games like Duck-Duck-Goose or Red Light-Green Light. Now that you're older yet, you're still playing games, but now maybe you play baseball or card games. Grownups also play games. So do very old people. Human beings of all ages all around the world like to play games!

Why do people play games? For lots of reasons. Games give people a way to **interact** with each other, a way to enjoy being together. Sometimes people play games when they're bored. Games are also good for the body and for the mind. Everybody plays games for different reasons at different times.

When did all of this playing begin? What was the first game and who played it? We don't really know. People have been playing games for a very long time. Games are a part of our *folklore*. They get passed along from parents to children. Games also get passed between children. They spread from kid to kid on playgrounds. Sometimes kids make up games on the spot. But most of the games we play have been around for hundreds of years. We don't usually know who invented them. They're folk games.

Games Are Good for You!

When you play games, you learn that it's fun to be with other people. You learn how to take turns and to trust others. Those are all important lessons for later on in life.

Some scientists have studied kids who play games. Kids who play more games often know how to solve problems better later on. They can also be more creative. They have good ideas.

Children teach each other games when they're playing together. These are folk games.

Games from Different Places and Different Times

Games don't have to be fancy or complicated. Some of the best games are played without much equipment. Jumping rope, for example, is a game that only requires one piece of rope. It's an old game that's been around a long time. Children today still enjoy it as much as they ever did.

Games come from around the world. They traveled to North America with *immigrants*. Kids who came from other countries shared their games with the children they met in North America. Then everyone started playing them.

For example, hopscotch has roots in parts of Africa. There are versions of this game in Zimbabwe and South Africa. There, people call it *tsetsetse*. They draw a rectangular grid on the ground. Then they put a stone in one square. Players hop on one foot and try to kick the stone into the next square. African slaves probably brought the game to North America. White children learned to play it from black children. Children all across North America still play hopscotch today.

Marbles is another very old game. It was one of the most popular kids' games back 200 years ago.

Red Rover

Red Rover is a game that was first played in England during the 1800s. Then it spread to the United States, Canada, and Australia. Sometimes it's also called Forcing the City Gates or Octopus Tag.

The game is played between two lines of players who stand about thirty feet apart. Each team lines up along one of these lines with their hands linked. The game starts when the first team calls out, "Red rover, red rover, send so-and-so over" Then the person whose name was called has to run to the other line and try to break through the other team's chain. If that person can't break through the line, she joins the other team. If she does break through, though, she can pick either of the two "links" (the children whose hands let go and broke the chain)

Young people playing Red Rover.

WHERE DO GAMES COME FROM?

Many times children's games come from actual historical events. For example, children used to play "cowboys-and-Indians" because they saw Western movies where white cowboys fought against Natives back in the days of the Wild West. Historians think that Red Rover might have started long, long ago, when the Vikings invaded England from the North. "Rover" was a Viking word that meant "pirate," so the English children who first played this game may have been showing their bravery by daring the enemy to "come over" the sea and attack them.

"IT"

Some games have each player doing the exact same thing. Other games have one player who is "It." For the time that the player is "It," that person does not perform the same activity as the other players. Here are two examples of "It" games played by immigrants from South America:

CABRA CEGA (BLIND NANNY GOAT)

"It" wears a blindfold as she or he tries to find the other children standing around. Those children try to escape from the blind nanny goat. When someone is touched by "It," the touched person becomes the new blind nanny goat.

TURKEY

A group of children stand in a circle. "It" stands in the middle. The children toss the ball to each other while trying to keep it away from the turkey. If the turkey ("It") catches the ball, she or he changes places with the child who threw it.

Can you think of any North American games that are like this?

A FOLK GAME FROM BRAZIL

In this South American country, children play a game called *gato mia* (cat meow). One child, who is blindfolded, has to find other children in a room. When the blindfolded child touches someone, she says, "Cat, meow." The touched child must meow, and the blindfolded child tries to guess who is the meowing child.

to come back with her and join her team. Then the other side does the same thing, until only one player is left on a team. If the last player can't break through the chain of children on the other side, then the other side wins.

Playing games is part of being a child. It's a way to learn and grow. Most children's games are folk games. No one knows who first played them. The rules aren't written down. These games just spread around the world, from playground to playground.

The games we play today are often versions of old games. We've changed them a little. But they're nothing new. We'll pass them on to the future. Kids a hundred years from now will probably be playing them.

TWO
Tag and Hide-and-Go-Seek

Do you and your friends ever play tag? How about hide-and-go-seek?

These are two of the most common games in the world. They are played all around the world. You don't need any equipment to play tag or hide-and-go-seek. You don't need to keep score. You don't need teams. These children's games are a part of the folklore of many, many countries.

In England and Ireland, tag is usually called "tig." Children in India play a game called landi taang. Each part of the world has its own versions of tag and hide-and-go-seek. Sometimes the two games run together into a single game.

Mr. Daruma Fell Down: Japanese Tag

In Japan, children playing outside are often playing Mr. Daruma Fell Down. Here's how they do it.

First, the person who is "It" yells to the other players, "Mr. Daruma fell down!" The other children run as far away as possible. Then "It" turns his back to the other players. He calls out again, "Mr.

Daruma fell down!" After that, he turns around and tries to catch the other children. If they stand still, he can't catch them, but if they move he can chase them and put them in "jail."

When "It's" back is turned and he is yelling, "Mr. Daruma fell down!" the other children run as fast as they can and try to touch his back before he turns around again. Whenever someone hits "It's" back, other children can escape from the jail.

These children are playing tag, a folk game that exists in many forms all around the world.

COMMANDER

Children in Taiwan play a game very like Mr. Daruma Fell Down—but they call it Commander. It is so popular that almost every child in Taiwan knows how to play it. First, one child is chosen to be a commander. She turns her back to everyone. Then she counts, "One . . . two . . . three!" Everyone moves closer to her while she's counting. After she finishes counting, she turns and looks at everyone. Nobody is allowed to move as long as she is looking. If somebody moves, the commander can point to that person and he is out. If someone is able to reach and touch the commander, he wins the game.

The Hunter:
Hide-and-Go-Seek from Saudi Arabia

In Saudi Arabia, in the Middle East, children play a game called Hunter. One child is chosen to be the hunter ("It"). She counts from one to ten with her eyes closed. Everyone else runs and hides somewhere. Then the hunter searches for the other children.

When the hunter finds someone, then the game turns into tag. If the player can run fast enough, he can get away from the hunter. But if the hunter touches him, then he is out.

When everyone is out, the first person who was caught becomes the next hunter.

Sardines: Hide-and-Go-Seek from Germany

German children play a game called Sardines. In this version of hide-and-go-seek, "It" is the person who hides. All the other children then look for her. Each time a player finds "It", he has to squeeze in next to wherever she's hiding and hide with her. The hiding spot gets more and more crowded. Eventually, the last person finds the entire group, and the game is over.

Catch the Chicks: Tag in Taiwan

Children who play this game in Taiwan pretend they are an eagle, a hen, and some chicks. All the chicks stand behind the hen in a row. The hen tries her best to protect her babies. When

BLIND MAN'S BUFF

Blind Man's Bluff is a little like tag—except "It" has to wear a blindfold. Back in the 1800s in England, this game used to be popular as a party game for adults. Variations of Blind Man's Bluff are played around the world. In Mexico, children play *Gallinita Ciega* (Blind Hen). In Germany, children play Blind Cow instead. Turkish children play *Korebe*.

the game starts, the eagle tries to catch the chicks. If the eagle catches a chick, then the eagle wins the game. The chick who is caught is the eagle in the next game.

Sun and Ice: Mexican Freeze Tag

Have you ever played freeze tag? In this kind of tag, if "It" touches you, you have to freeze. You can't move until someone else touches you.

FREEZE TAG IN OTHER PLACES

Freeze tag has other names in other places of the world. In various parts of Asia, it is known as Stuck in the Mud, Sticky-Glue, or Ice-and-Water. Players who are tagged are "stuck in the mud" or "frozen." They have to stand in place with their arms stretched out until they are unfrozen. An unstuck or unfrozen player has to "thaw" them or "unstick" them by crawling between their legs. In another variation, called Toilet Tag, the stuck players have to be "flushed" by another player hitting their outstretched hands. In the United States and Canada, kids sometimes play a type of freeze tag called TV Tag, where in order to unfreeze someone, the player must also call out the name of a TV show. Once called, that TV show can no longer be used to unfreeze someone again.

Children in Jerusalem playing with each other.

Children in Mexico play a game like this called Sun and Ice. Players form two teams. Then the two teams chase each other. If you touch someone on another team, you yell, "Ice!" and that person can't move. If someone on your own team touches you, though, she will yell, "Sun!" Then you can run again.

All Around the World

Children all around the world play games that are a lot alike. Maybe that's because human beings are pretty much the same, no matter where they live or what they look like. Games like tag and hide-and-go-seek are a part of folklore everywhere. They're just part of being a kid, no matter where . . . or when.

✳ THREE
Games Played with Balls

Lots of folk games can be played with absolutely no equipment. Some folk games use very simple equipment, though—like a rope for jump rope—or a ball. Many, many different kinds of folk games can be played with a ball. Balls have been a part of human play for thousands of years.

The History of the Ball

Long, long ago (about 2,000 years ago, in fact), the Chinese played a game called *tsu chu*. They used balls made out of animal skins to play this game. The balls had to be driven through gaps in a net stretched between two poles. The ancient Greeks and Romans also played a game where they kicked and carried a ball (a little like modern American football).

In the Middle Ages, about 1,000 years ago, when people killed an animal for its meat, they would blow up the animal's bladder like a balloon. Then they would play a game where they used their hands and feet to keep the "ball" up in the air (like the modern game of hacky sack).

South American Natives were the first to use a rubber ball that would bounce. The rest of the world didn't use rubber balls, though, until the 1800s. Most balls were still made out of animal skins until the 20th century, when rubber balls really caught on.

Many ball games eventually turned into the sports we play today. These are organized games with written rules. They have their roots in folk games, but their modern versions are no longer thought of as folk games. Football, soccer, basketball, and baseball all have their roots in very old games that were passed along from person to person and from generation to generation.

But children still play folk games that use balls. Dodge ball is one of these games. So is keep-away and monkey-in-the-middle. Children in other parts of the world play other folk games that use balls.

Oba: A Ball Game from Colombia

Oba is a game that children play on playgrounds in Colombia. They throw a ball against a wall, but as they do so, they have

Balls and children just go together!

to do it a different way each time, while singing a song that goes along with the game. Sometimes they have to throw the ball with one arm, sometimes with two arms. Sometimes they have to stand on one leg while they throw the ball. Or they have to jump up and down while they throw it. Then they have to catch the ball when it bounces back, all the while singing the song. Kids end up giggling a lot. The harder they laugh, the harder it is for them to catch the ball.

Keep the Ball: A Mexican Game

Children in Mexico sometimes play a game called Keep the Ball. First they form two teams. One child is chosen to keep time and they decide on how long they will play. It could be ten minutes or fifteen minutes or half an hour. The game starts when somebody throws the ball up to the sky. The player who catches the ball has to keep the ball for his team. He has to throw the ball to other people on his team. Meanwhile, each person on the opposite team has to try to steal the ball. When someone throws you the ball, you can't throw it back to the same person. You have to throw it to a different person. When the person how is keeping track of the time yells, "Stop!" whichever team has the ball wins.

Baseball Folklore

Baseball is called America's favorite game. It isn't a folk game. But it started out as a folk game. Historians think that a folk game called stoolball was one of the earliest forms of baseball. This was a game that was played in England. It was being played about 800 years ago.

To play stoolball a batter stood in front of an upturned stool, while another player pitched a ball to the batter. If the batter hit the ball (either with a bat or with her hand) and another player caught it, the batter was out. If the pitched ball hit a stool leg, the batter was out. Milkmaids used to play this game. They used their milking stools.

A lot of folk *traditions* have also grown around baseball. The game takes a long time, but people have fun through the

Baseball is a professional sport, but its roots lie in ancient folk games.

whole thing. The traditions are part of what make it so fun. In the United States, before the game begins, everyone stands up and sings the "Star-Spangled Banner." Fans try to catch stray balls. Between innings, kids run races around the bases against the mascots. People eat special foods like hot dogs and peanuts. During the "seventh-inning stretch," everyone sings "Take Me Out to the Ball Game."

CANADA'S NATIONAL SPORT

In 1867, Canada decided that lacrosse was its national sport. That's still true today. Lacrosse started out as a folk game, though. Native North Americans invented it.

Native people often played games with balls. In the eastern part of America, a ball game was popular called baggataway. It was played with sticks that had a loop on one end with a net fastened to it. The net was used to catch the ball. French Canadians first used the term la crosse to refer to this playing stick.

Lacrosse is not just played in Canada. Though not as well known as some other sports, Americans have also played it since the late 1800s. Today it is played on many college campuses.

Balls Forever

Kids have been throwing, kicking, and catching things for thousands of years. Before they had balls, they used vegetables and stones. Sometimes they even used animal skulls. Then they used tin cans. They used balls made of leather.

Rubber made balls even more fun. Balls that could bounce made games more interesting. People invented new games that couldn't have been played with a ball that didn't bounce.

Native North Americans played a game with balls and nets on sticks. Today, we call this game lacrosse.

No matter how many new things are invented, people will still play with balls. Our world will never get so modern that we get tired of ball games!

FOUR
Indoor Games

Words to Understand

A *variation* is a change or small difference from one thing to another.

Archeologists are people who study human life from a long time ago by finding and looking at the various objects and buildings long-ago people left behind.

Generations are all the people born at about the same time. Your grandparents are one generation, your parents and aunts and uncles are another generation, and you, your brothers and sisters, and your cousins are another.

We play a lot of games outside. But sometimes we can't. Maybe it's raining. Or we live somewhere really cold, and we spend a lot the time indoors. Does that mean we can't play any games? Of course not!

There are lots of games to play inside. In the past, sitting together and playing games around a table was something people did a lot. People played games when they had visitors. Or when it was too dark outside to keep working or playing. Or when it was raining.

Today, we still play lots of games inside. Maybe you even have a family board game night where your whole family plays your favorite games. You might play games like Monopoly® or Scrabble®. Maybe you play computer games. These types of games aren't folk games. But maybe you play cards or guessing games. Both of these are folk games.

ANCIENT BOARD GAMES

Some board games we play today are actually folk games. They've been around for thousands of years. No one knows who first invented them. The rules were passed along from person to person for centuries before they were ever written down. Backgammon, for example, was played in the Middle East more than 5,000 years ago. People in ancient Greece and Egypt played a game that looked like checkers. A game like chess was invented about 1,500 years ago in the Middle East. A thousand years ago, the game spread to Europe, and by the 1400s, the rules were pretty much the same as they are today.

Card Games

Cards have been around for a long, long time. More than a thousand years ago, the ancient Chinese first invented this game. Five hundred years later, playing cards spread around the Earth to Europe. By the 1700s, playing cards had become a popular game in the United States. And playing cards is still one of the all-time favorite indoor games.

Card games have been around for hundreds of years.

Old Maid is one very old card game. It's all about matching pairs. It's a good game for young kids to play. Children in England in the 1800s first played Old Maid, but matching card games like Old Maid are even older than that. Games that have the same rules as Old Maid are also played all around the world. Many countries have their own *variation* of this game. Children in the Middle East play a game called "Blind King." Children in Japan play a game like Old Maid called *baba-nuki*. In Brazil, there's a game like Old Maid called Stink.

Dice Games

Lots of modern board games use dice. But dice have been around for more than 5,000 years. **Archeologists** have found them in ancient ruins in the Middle East and in India.

DECKS OF CARDS

Cards haven't always looked the same. Today there are 52 cards in a deck. In other countries, decks have fewer cards. We have four suites: hearts, clubs, spades, and diamonds. At other times in history, people have used other objects, like elephants, birds, leaves, and flowers.

Dice are a very ancient game.

The dice we usually use today have six sides, but dice come in different shapes. Games played with two-sided dice were popular among some groups of Native Americans. People in different parts of the world also used four-sided dice and pyramid-shaped dice.

Games like dice and cards are found everywhere, all around the world. They're a part of the human memory. These ancient games will be passed on to new **generations**.

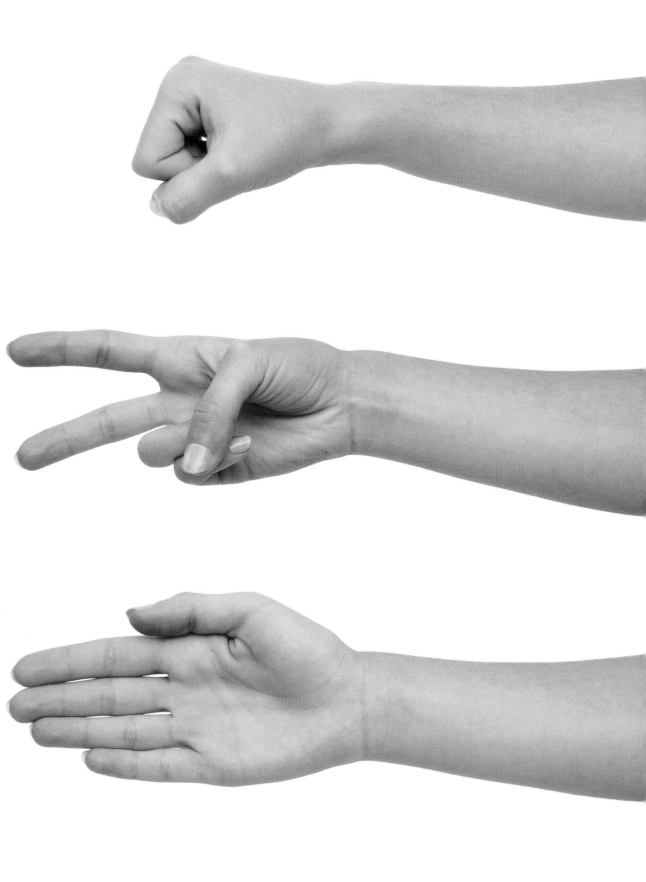

✳ FIVE
Games for
Small Spaces

What do you do on a long car ride? Do you play a game with your family?

That's what a lot of kids do. If they're sitting in car, they need a game that doesn't take up a lot of space. They can't run around, obviously! They can't use a board game very easily. And they can't throw a ball.

All sorts of folk games can be played on long car rides. Here are a few of them:

- Rock, paper, scissors is a game you can play with two people and just your hands. To play this, each player makes a fist and says out loud, "Rock, paper, scissors," swinging down his fist with each word. After the third word, each player makes one of three hand gestures: a closed fist stands for "rock," an open hand means "paper," and two fingers in a V stands for "scissors." Since a rock can dull a pair of scissors, rock beats scissors. Scissors cut paper, so scissors beat paper. Since paper can cover a rock, paper beats rock. If both people use the same gesture, the game is tied.

DID YOU KNOW?

Rock, paper, scissors is played in many countries. It is called *Jan Ken Po* in Japan, where it has been played for centuries.

- I Spy is another good game for a car ride. One person in the car chooses an object inside the car. She then gives the other people in the car a clue by saying, "I spy with my little eye, something . . ." She then says the object's color, gives the first letter of the name of the object, or says another clue. The person who guesses the object correctly is the next person to spy a new item.
- Cat's cradle is a string game that can be played between two people sitting side by side in the car. It's a folk game that's been around for a long time. Historians think the game may have started thousands of years ago in China or Korea.

DID YOU KNOW?

People all around the world play string games. The Native people of North America say that Grandmother Spider taught them to play weaving games.

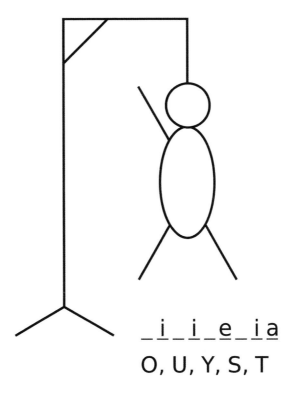

_ i _ i _ e _ i a

O, U, Y, S, T

- If you have a paper and pencil in the car, you can play a folk game called hangman. It's a letter game that's probably been around since the 1800s.
- When you get tired of hangman, you can use your paper and pencil to play tic-tac-toe. This game is at least 2,000 years old. The ancient Egyptians and the ancient Romans used to play it. In the 1800s in England, children played the same game—but they called it "naught and crosses."

All these games can be played anywhere. They don't have to be played on a car ride. Instead, they can be played on the

Children learn how to get along with each other by playing games together.

NEW FOLK GAMES?

Computer games can be played with strangers from across the world over the Internet. Some computer games are created and sold—but users make others. No one really knows who first made them. Then they spread from player to player. In a way, they're the newest form of folk games.

playground or in a classroom. They can be played on a rainy afternoon when you're stuck inside. They can even be played when you're sick in bed!

Some games are competitive. That means you try to win. Other games aren't. They help people work together. Some games mostly use your body. Or games can mostly use your mind. Others use both.

Games help us in all sorts of ways. They help us get exercise and make friends. They teach us how to solve problems and work together.

But most important, games are fun! Both kids and adults play games all the time. They've been playing the same games for hundreds of years, inventing new variations all the time. Games are a part of our folklore. They've always been a part of human life—and they always will be.

Find Out More

In Books

Chetwynd, Josh. *The Secret History of Balls: The Stories Behind the Things We Love to Catch, Whack, Throw, Kick, Bounce and Bat.* New York: Perigee, 2011.

Gryski, Camilla. *Let's Play: Traditional Games of Childhood.* Toronto: Kids Can Press, 2007.

Jara, Alicia Sanchez. *Juegos y Cantos: Traditional Mexican Games and Songs.* Mexico D.F.: Editorial Trillas, 2009.

On the Internet

Children's Folk Games
www.estcomp.ro/~cfg/games.html

Folk Games
digital.library.okstate.edu/encyclopedia/entries/F/FO007.html

Index

Picture Credits

About the Author and the Consultant

Gus Snedeker is proud of his heritage as a Dutch American. He loves to study the stories and traditions of the various groups of people who helped build America. He has also written several other books in this series.

Dr. Alan Jabbour is a folklorist who served as the founding director of the American Folklife Center at the Library of Congress from 1976 to 1999. Previously, he began the grant-giving program in folk arts at the National Endowment for the Arts (1974-76). A native of Jacksonville, Florida, he was trained at the University of Miami (B.A.) and Duke University (M.A., Ph.D.). A violinist from childhood on, he documented old-time fiddling in the Upper South in the 1960s and 1970s. A specialist in instrumental folk music, he is known as a fiddler himself, an art he acquired directly from elderly fiddlers in North Carolina, Virginia, and West Virginia. He has taught folklore and folk music at UCLA and the University of Maryland and has published widely in the field.